I0844955

"This is for my dear Alicia.
Keep asking all the questions
because curiosity is the path of adventure
that leads to discoveries."
Catarina Cunha

ALICIA'S DISCOVERIES

Catching a Rainbow

By Catarina Cunha

Illustrated by Megumi Arai

Alicia looked out of the window.
Rain again?

Alicia was upset.
She really wanted to ride her bicycle.

She decided to do it anyway.
She got her rain gear, put it on,
and out she went.

She rode through mud and splashed in puddles.
Alicia shouted cheerfully.
"This is even better than on sunny days!"

Just then the clouds let some sun through.
And there it was, a beautiful rainbow!

Alicia marveled at it, and decided to catch it.

She pedaled and pedaled to get closer, but it didn't work.

Why couldn't she catch it?

After trying and trying again,
Alicia was frustrated and hungry.

Alicia went back inside. Alicia thought to herself:
"My mom is a scientist; she has an answer for sure."

Alicia asked: "Mom, I saw a rainbow outside!
Why can't I catch it? What is a rainbow?"

Alicia's mom smiled and answered:
"Alicia, a rainbow is colored light that you see in the sky
when sun rays shine on falling raindrops."

Alicia said: "But mom, they look like magic bridges!"
Alicia's mom: "That is because the raindrops that
reflect the sunlight are curved.
A rainbow is actually a circle and has no end."

"Which colors did you see?"
Alicia tried to remember: "I saw red, orange..."
Alicia's mom continued: "...Yellow, green, blue,
indigo and violet."

"Wait, we have a prism somewhere in my office,
with it, we can create our own rainbow
and maybe draw it.
This way you can look at your picture every day.
That is sort of catching a rainbow isn't it?"
Alicia smiled: "That is a great idea!
Let's do it right now!"

That was the day Alicia caught a rainbow.
How about you catch your own rainbow today?

Enjoy!

How to make a rainbow

[Version 1]

You will need
- A shallow pan with water
- A flashlight or Sunlight
- A white surface or piece of paper

[Version 2]

You will need
- A CD
- A flashlight

easy to do!